the surprising role of systems in the health of
church staff and key leaders

Wayne Stewart

FLOW: the surprising role of systems in the health of church staff and key leaders

Copyright © 2019 Wayne Stewart

wayne.stewart@waynecstewart.com

CONTENTS

May 1990:

The first images came back and everyone knew
something was wrong. Very wrong.

A few weeks into low Earth orbit, the Hubble Space Telescope
had produced nothing more than grainy distortions. She was,
and remains, the most sophisticated scientific instrument ever
focused on the cosmos. Given decades of attention and serious
funding—eventually topping out at 4.7 billion—this was not supposed to
happen.

The technical term was spherical aberration. The actual flaw? An edge
of Hubble's nearly 8ft across lens, off by 2200 nanometers.

2.2 micrometers. 87 microinches.

Less than 1/50 of a hair's width.

Hard to catch, especially when the measurements showed true. It turns
out a testing device had been improperly assembled, again at a very
slight inconsistency, this time 1.3mm. More than enough. While hard to
believe that the world's premiere agency in the business of scientific
precision could make such an error, the same would happen if a builder
spec'd an 8ft. high wall, using a tape measure with a foot indicated every
13 inches.

They didn't see it. Until they saw it.

But the end of the story, at least so far, is a happy one. Three years were spent devising and training for the fix. While in orbit, NASA initiated a space-walk repair amounting to the installation of some very high-tech contact lenses. And what a repair it was. Given regular update missions, the last in 2014, we've received images of the universe we never thought possible, and learned more than we ever imagined.

The heavens declare the glory of God.

And now we get to see this truth (and the heavens) with ever increasing clarity and beauty because—and this is very important—though the problem seemed small and likely difficult to diagnose, the men and women of NASA were absolutely committed to reversing its affects and releasing the promise that Hubble presented.

Okay.

Let's make the shift to church. Your church. My church. The Church.

And more specifically, your church staff and key leaders.

Sometimes ministry feels like a grainy distortion. We know something's wrong. That's obvious. It's also frustrating. What did we do? What didn't we do? And what's next, especially when we've done all we know how.

The conversation unfolding in these pages is dedicated to those very questions, the idea that some measure of your challenges may be related to dynamics you've yet to "see", and the hope that knowing where to look (and a little bit of what to do about it) can make a big difference for the ongoing health and vibrancy of your staff and key leaders.

Fall 2019

Resistance

As protective measure or moral stance:
necessary, honorable.
Among church staff and volunteer leaders?
Not so much.

Think of your church staff and key volunteer leaders as a light bulb, fully lit. Glowing. Spreading. Spilling light across the room. What might this look like? The Word: informing and shaping interactions. The joyful Family of God living out its calling. The presence, gifts, and fruit of the Spirit—on full display and in use. Grace in misunderstandings and reconciliation for hurts. Hope and energy towards a collective future. Transformation. It's an exciting proposition, not unlike our earliest images from the Book of Acts.

Now think of your staff and leaders as a light bulb, partially lit. Intermittent. That last cycle-on before the filament pops. One can imagine how this might appear as well. Deadlines passing, with key ministry initiatives held up "somewhere." Staff and leader missteps in communication. Lack of trust or willingness to collaborate. Silos. A serious downshift in momentum and teamsmanship and a surprising lack of emotional margin.

Something's not right.

In electrical circuitry language, there's something hindering—resisting— that free flow of energy. To be fair to the metaphor, some resistance is a good thing, just like physical strain builds muscle when faced with opposing force. But that's not what's going on here. The church-circuit isn't designed to induce strain. God may use this type of thing for our transformation but I don't know a pastor that actually designs church-life as an intentional struggle for staff and key leaders.

No, things just don't seem to be flowing.

When we sit down to reflect on it, we're likely naming these problems as a lack of unity and mission effectiveness. People are not pulling together on the rope. They may or may not be fighting, but they are certainly not co-laboring in a manner consistent with New Testament ideals. And so we think, "Is this it? Are we actually making a difference for the Kingdom? Or are we just putting on a decent presentation weekly?"

But here's what is right.

The vast majority of church staff and pastors I know are not going to let this bulb flicker. Being church people, we investigate where we're most comfortable: relationships, ideas, programming.

Outstanding. But have you found that one more sit down, one more level-setting conversation, one more ministry post-mortem, one more SWOT procedure[1] just hasn't moved the needle? Do they matter? Absolutely.

Did they resolve the issue?

Let me ask: what if at least a portion of this non-flow problem lies in a deeper and perhaps yet simpler, place? What if the resistance you're experiencing is coming from somewhere you haven't yet looked? Or simply feel ill-equipped to look? And what if our people-program-idea efforts actually lead us to some errant people-program-idea decisions? Church systems author John Wimberly raises a troubling thought:

> "... when it comes to personnel issues, an individualistic approach often leads to false solutions and misidentified problems. By focusing on individuals, not systems, congregations, almost invariably, blame individuals for troubles that may in fact be more systemic." [2]

That would be tragic. And a significant failure of our incarnational duty to one another.

Here's my pitch.

Some measure of your flow-challenges may be related to church systems issues, specifically, what we might call church macro-systems.

Two Scripture settings come to mind: Ex. 18:13-27 and Acts 6:1-7.

One tells the story of an overburdened justice system. The other presents a felt-needs delivery model in disrepair. Both are resolved by godly concern and the restructuring of the systems in question. Caring wasn't enough. I know, that sounds harsh. The first step was caring. The second step was caring enough to do something about it.

Moses humbly received corrective input and then did something. The Apostles received a critique regarding the early Church's social support net and then did something. In both cases, new workflows, leadership, and expectations won the day. Led by godly, Spirit-infused wisdom, more and more people gained a timely hearing and resolution of grievances, and in the second case, women already suffering great loss were reminded of their immense value in quite tangible ways.

Not surprisingly, these principles surface outside the church walls as well.

In a podcast interview titled "A Process for Process" guest Robert Sfeir lets us in on his passion for this kind of work. As Senior Director of Engineering at Huge, Mr. Sfeir manages systems for this digital content agency of 1500 creatives and producers. That's a bit to keep moving in the right direction. Here's his vision:

> *"I love being able to introduce so much effectiveness into a process that people get time to breathe, people get time to think..."* [3]

Breathe.

Think.

Is this the way your staff and key volunteers would describe the good work of ministry at your church? If not, have you noticed them gasping or a bit fuzzy?

The effectiveness Mr. Sfeir seeks is not for the sake of the systems themselves. His goal is to make things flow, with people the beneficiaries, enjoying (metaphorically) two of the most basic things for which they were created. To "breathe and think" is a glorious vision.

Flow is the goal.

And a pebble in my shoe, while insignificant in size, might cause enough irritation that I stop to bend down in the middle of the road...

Pastor, church leader, please:

Fix what *can* be fixed. Persevere in love through the rest.[4]

First up: exactly what is a church macro-system, and how would I know if ours are in disrepair?

Ideas and Questions

What is a church macro-system?
How would I know if ours are in disrepair?

Definition 1: church macro-systems

Workflows and tools used globally to facilitate time, space, equipment, production, and communication in your church organization. Everyone uses them. They are the ways everyone gets work done, together.

Right away you can imagine that some measure of brokenness in something everyone uses all the time will spread that measure of brokenness to... well, everyone. Seems simple, right?

Definition 2: your church organization

Paid staff and key volunteer leaders. Congregants not in key leadership will certainly reap the rewards of this kind of work. They're just not the target demographic for our particular concerns.

Definition 3: church macro-systems capacities

In the church world, macro-systems largely engage and manage three key_5 capacities:

- Operations (the physical environments in which ministry leaders do their programs).

- Tech (the tools and skilled operators that ministry leaders often need to present their programs), and

- Communication (how ministry leaders promote vision/events and recruit teams).

So, how are you doing?

Use the descriptors and scales from left to right.

1) What occupies your key resource capacities (ops, tech, comm): ministry/department events or church-wide vision/strategy?

(1,2,3,4)

2) Does your church communication feel more like: an endless string of unrelated information or a cohesive whole with compelling action steps?

(1,2,3,4)

3) Do your support teams: feel overwhelmed and unsure of when the next big priority will hit (and how to navigate what's already in the queue) or feel they can work a plan and understand its strategic value?

(1,2,3,4)

4) Do your ministry leads: feel frustrated with the level of support they receive or experience support teams as joyful partnership?

(1,2,3,4)

5) Do ministry projects: seem to wander to implementation (or quiet death) or culminate in a known win for everyone involved?

(1,2,3,4)

6) Do you more often think of challenges in the three key capacities: as "tensions to be managed" or "problems to be solved?"

(1,2,3,4)

Somewhere in the high teens to low twenties would indicate a relatively greater presence of flow. Below that could indicate a somewhat greater presence of resistance. Where did you land? Find anything worth uncovering a bit more? Any capacities scoring consistently higher or lower? With these as conversation starters, let's lay some important groundwork.

Good macro-systems are:

Knowable (everyone using the system can summarize its basic structure)

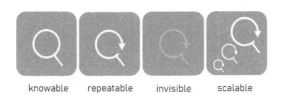

knowable   repeatable   invisible   scalable

It stands to reason that the ways everyone gets work done together need to be understood by everyone. But that's not always the case. It's maybe not even all that often the case in church organizations.

Why? Getting to understandable structures and language is a very challenging discipline. We understand this when it comes to theology. The same relentless pursuit of the irreducible and compelling should apply to our systems. Can it be talked about in common terms that land with the appropriate implications? That's the standard.

Repeatable (everyone can do the work with the same tools and steps)

When do systems fail? When they require new or different steps for different users.

Invisible (eventually—they'll seem ever-present during development but good macro-systems fade well)

You may not believe me on this one (especially as you engage new systems work), but given time all systems will fade into the background of ministry life. New systems work takes up an inordinate amount of time and energy, elevating initially what is meant to run in the background. It's perfectly normal, if a bit maddening. Which leads to our last descriptor.

Scalable (can go up or down in numbers of people or tasks without affecting stated outcomes)

Appropriately designed systems can account for increased or

decreased people and tasks without a complete overhaul. One direction (decrease) is a focus. One (increase) is an expansion. Both are measures of scale. If the basic structure of the system must be skewed (or destroyed) in order to scale, you will be coming back to ground zero far more than is healthy.

Our Scriptural Context

While the NT talks consistently about unity and its mission-enabling presence, one text holds particular relevance for our conversation and process.

Eph. 4:2 says,

> "Be completely humble and gentle; be patient, bearing with one another in love. Make every effort to keep the unity of the Spirit through the bond of peace."

We might be tempted to read this as just one more call for unity in the Body, but tellingly it lands right in the middle of Paul's dissertation on gifts and roles the Spirit has placed into the Church for her health and mission.

Apostles. Prophets. Evangelists. Pastors. Teachers.

If it is this group's responsibility to help foster and develop a "unity in the faith and knowledge of the Son of God" then the relational and spiritual posture of a disciple is surely to be lived out by discipler.

- Humility and gentleness: because systems work brings change

- Patience: because systems take time to develop and even longer to become the status quo

- Bear with one another in love: because we will have missteps along the way

- Make every effort: because these issues can largely be addressed and the outcomes are well worth it

I've been in quite a few settings where ministry leaders bring attention to operations, tech, and communications staff, publicly and positively calling out their efforts. Usually after a hard run at a busy season or major event. The intent is good. A thank you for the extra mile to a group not often thanked in public. Any guess as to how many of those folks walk out of the room still contemplating resignation?

Far more than we'd like to know.

It's not that they don't appreciate a thank you. But when outsized expectations, miscommunication, and chaotic workflow brought them to the edge and then the edge wasn't moved any further going forward, what do we expect?

I've sat through a number of key volunteer leader "exits." Sometimes the desire to find another church home was related to doctrinal issues. But sometimes it was a measure of disconnect between how healthy organizations function and what they experienced in our setting. It made no sense to them that they enjoyed better unity, collaboration, and mission effectiveness at their workplace or other community concern. These people get good things done in their weekly places of influence. They found barriers at our church and looked for a different place to use their gifts.

Lastly, I've also been on the ministry leader side of the equation. No matter what I did, it didn't matter. I'd plan in advance. Try to account for every variable. Extra, extra emails and face to face.

What was I missing?

The simple fact that, while I had executed some good planning and conversation, my planning and conversation was coming at support staff and key volunteer leaders in a slightly different manner than the ten other people coming at them with planning and conversation. Just enough to make ten different workflows and ten different relational tangles. These folks are especially aware of the unspoken hierarchies of ministry leadership. If you happen to be nearer the "top" of that pile, your planning and conversation not only comes with your particular style and tools, it also comes with a heavier load of urgency.

> **"... when outsized expectations, miscommunication, and chaotic workflow brought them to the edge and then the edge wasn't moved any further going forward, what do we expect?"**

Just like Moses and the Apostles, and much like the vision of Robert Sfeir, when we address our church organization's unnecessary resistance, we grow into a more unified and mission-effective flow. Good things happen when we breathe freely, when we think clearly and creatively. Far from being restrictive, good church macro-systems might be the piece you're missing.

You've Got This

Yes, we are about to dive into some deeper weeds, and largely in fields where you spend little time regularly. But here's the call: it's really important. And half the job is something you're already quite good at. While the next chapters are largely the *why* and *how to build* of macrosystems, these steps fall flat without your leadership. Inspiring. Teaching. Showing the way forward. Listening. Praying. You know, pastoring and leading a staff team and key volunteers. The stuff you do really well, all the time.

On a very practical note, don't let the nitty gritty slow you down from completing these brief sixty-two pages. When you encounter a system or structure that doesn't immediately click, just make a note and keep moving. It's extremely important to complete the principles to make a judgment as to whether or not some of the (much harder) systems design work will be of benefit. And there's plenty of examples and stories along the way to help when the details feel fuzzy. They will.

But be encouraged. You can do this.

Ready? Let's head into what I'll call the Big Three of church macrosystems while focusing on the people outcomes we dearly long to see.

Project management. Planning rhythms. Resource use.

James

Most Mondays were a challenge.
This one pushed him to the edge.

 He stared at his inbox. For quite some time.

Three particular messages—from three different senders—took
their toll.

"James,

*Thanks so much for your hard work on the Easter Celebration
outreach mailer. Looks like we can just squeeze it in in time. Please
use whatever text you think will work and run with it. We'll figure out
the costs later..."*

───────────

"James,

*I just found out we're running a mailer for Easter? How much are we
spending? What budget was that approved from? I'll need to see it
soon and I've attached some thoughts... "*

───────────

"James (and leadership team),

I just saw the draft and am concerned we've not had broader staff input on the Easter mailer. It seems like something we'd all want to be in on. Are we just highlighting services? What about the Kids Fair? The Students Service Day is a perfect example of the resurrection and Gospel in action. Are the lillies still for purchase in memorium?... "

———————

He blinked.

Nope, still there.

Project Management:
The Hidden People Issue

Church isn't about projects. It's about people.
Surprise. It's filled with both.

Wikipedia describes project management as an orderly approach to work "... typically relating to the construction industry, architecture, aerospace and defense, computer networking, telecommunications or software development."[5]

Our first bump in the road?

Churches don't make the list.

The fine people writing this definition didn't have "church" pop into their minds while considering project management's most obvious applications. How often does the subject surface in your ministry conversations or meetings? I would venture rarely. Maybe never. And for good reason. Men and women don't enter ministry to manage projects. They want to honor God and care for people.

Got it.

But, what about a weekend service and its multitude of details? What about a seasonal initiative including a musical production or special platform decor? A great video to tell someone's salvation story? Children's camp or VBS? Building campaign or stewardship celebration evening? A book or devotional produced by your Lead Pastor or team?

Podcast? Worship Album? Short-Term Mission Trips? Visuals and build -up for a new teaching series? And what about changes in systems themselves? New database or scheduling software? Giving platforms? Ministry planning rhythms? Alternate service on the horizon or expansion to a multi-site model?

"Oh," you say. "You mean admin. Yeah, we all have to do it from time to time. It's not our favorite but it's part of ministry life."

Bingo.

Our first challenge is that churches don't realize the degree to which project management is in the air. The second hill to take is just as prevalent and more slippery on the way up: the mis-categorization of project management as administration. At some level this is semantics. On a whole other level, a crucial distinction in reducing unnecessary resistance. Three thoughts and a visual may help.

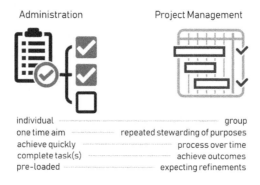

Administration	Project Management
individual	group
one time aim	repeated stewarding of purposes
achieve quickly	process over time
complete task(s)	achieve outcomes
pre-loaded	expecting refinements

First, administration largely concerns itself with accuracy, efficiency, and completion. "By myself and as quickly as possible" can be the ministry mindset for administrative tasks. Some of this is absolutely necessary. Not so with the church "projects" listed above. They require many hands, many voices. Administration can be accomplished by one person fairly quickly. Projects, for the most part, cannot. Confusing the two is never a good thing.

Next, projects fly or fail based on the careful and consistent stewarding of desired outcomes. How will ordering new candle holders for Christmas Eve (more an administrative task) demonstrably affect relationships, unity, or discipleship? Not sure there's much to spend time on there. But that Christmas Eve Service video? Its impact will largely be proportional to its process, which is always driven by its purposes. Those purposes will need to remain front and center. It's far too easy to wander off-point.

Lastly, projects exhibit a key relationship to time and input. While involving a set of tasks, projects are not merely the completion of those tasks. In real-world situations, and especially ministry life, projects are a rhythm of conversations and achievements all heading in the same direction and—importantly—subject to refinements as needed.

Faithful administration is critical in a church, especially one growing in size or complexity. Healthy project management, even more so. Why? Because projects live at the place where people collide or collaborate. It's really our choice.

Here's the people-gains we can experience when giving resources and attention to healthy project management within the church

Unity. Good church macro-systems help the hard work of ministry by facilitating a less-charged atmosphere. It's easy to see if we simply apply our four aspects of a good macro-system. When was the last time you were in a church workgroup where the process was knowable, repeatable, invisible, and scalable? That seems like a place of minimal friction, great flow, and rich in relationship and outcomes. Good project management helps calm the waters. When that's the case, more people show up to your pool party.

Missional Alignment and Energy. Good project management is good shepherding. It recognizes important Kingdom gains as hard-fought battles, requiring constant reinforcement of the *what for* in ways that motivate powerfully. It's the reason battle standards carry imagery, often family crests or regimental icons— a crucial reminder of what we're here for and what it is we stand to lose. Set and keep a workgroup's clear path (or their only path) to victory. Watch what happens.

Right-Sized Input and Decisions. It seems that churches move fast on the input and decisions of a few or very, very slow on the input and decisions of many. Neither is healthy or sustainable. And neither recognizes: A) all true projects require multiple voices but do not require every voice, and B) all true projects require the "right" amount of steps and time to achieve desired outcomes. Some initiatives require more people and steps than others.

Healthy collaboration and cross-checking requires wisdom and experience about who should be on the team.

Telling the Story of Wins: Momentum. In baseball, a player sliding across home plate a split second before the catcher places the tag is exhilarating. But the umpire's extended arms tell the actual outcome. Good project management signals the win in a way that is obvious and can be celebrated.

> ## "Projects live at the place where people collide or collaborate. It's really our choice."

So, here's the not-so-secret secret: project management in the Church is not about projects. It's about things of the Kingdom. Eternal things. At its best, project management in the Church keeps us on target with the things of God as the people of God.

Colin Ellis, project management and organizational culture writer and thinker, moves us in this direction when he says:

> *"... it's who you are as a person and the environment you create for others to do great work that will make you successful as a project manager."[6]*

But being a project manager is not enough. And making the leap from project manager to project leader is so much more than new systems or training:

> *"... it's easier for organisations to send everyone on a certification course so they can tick a 'We've spent money on improving the way we deliver projects' box than it is to set a new standard for behaviour... Leadership is not a program, though. It's making a series of choices that demonstrate the courage to do things differently. To challenge the status quo. To invest in people and team building, and to have the discipline to get things done."[7]*

Sounds an awful lot like pastoring and discipleship, right?

But it's not all sunshine and unicorns, as they say. Let's touch on the five biggest challenges to project management in the Church:

1. No one knows it's a thing requiring attention. But you're reading this so #1 solved. Move on.

2. Lead Pastor and/or elder board buy-in. What can I say? The extent to which key leaders are champions and practitioners of your project management structures is the extent to which it will help reduce unnecessary systems resistance, introducing the gains we highlighted. I dare say it's a 1:1 correlation.

3. Communicating and adopting new rhythms and standards. Basic change management here. Always dicey. Be patient.

4. Overly homogeneous staffing personality. And you thought it was neat that 90% of your staff holds the same Enneagram profile...

5. The art of caring for people while keeping things moving. Pastoral leadership at its finest, folks. Don't apologize for slowing down to treat the wounded or push at the edges because you know they can take that next hill.

Okay. Lots to gain. Much to consider.

Let's look at how you might improve your church's approach to project management by learning a basic pm structure.

Project Management:
A Suggested Approach

5 signposts. 4 phases. 3 versions.
2 or more circles of input.
1 really great project.

Standards for how a project comes to be, how to invite people into the work, and how to know when we've done the thing are crucial elements to ministry impact. People just function better when they know what's coming, when it's coming, and what they're supposed to do with it. Here's one structure to consider and then modify to match your church and leadership DNA.

Let's start with five signposts and the four phases they traverse:

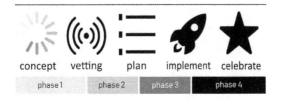

- Phase 1: From concept to vetting.

- Phase 2: Vetting to plan.

- Phase 3: Plan to implementation.

- Phase 4: Celebrate and Adjust.

Now let's talk about versions. Very straightforward:

- Version 1 is a sketch that initiates conversation.

- Version 2 moves the idea forward and has as many iterations and adjustments as needed.

- Version 3 is the greenlighted plan.

Lastly, our circles are just people. Groups of people.

- Circle 1: the core workgroup for the project.

- Circle 2: additional voices, especially those directly impacted by project outcomes.

- Circle 3: those with an indirect connection to project outcomes but a sphere of influence or experience related to the project, ie—interested professionals in your congregation or community.

4 phases. 3 versions. 2 (or more) circles of input.

Let's walk through the progression.

In the Beginning—

… was a v1 draft. One page—more bullets than paragraphs—and addressing:

Vision. What gain will we celebrate upon accomplishment?

Outline. Broad sketch ready for input. Time spent developing should represent both general nature but also any pre-established non-negotiables. Cover the basics of what, how, when, whom, how much?

Challenges. What initial challenges do you see? List no more than three.

People. Who will help you refine this draft and move on to a Version 2?

Here's a recent v1 I produced to start a conversation around strategic communication at our church:

****

Christ Community Church

Process and Project Worksheet

V1

Process/Project Title: Strategic Communications Refinement

Initiated by/date: WCS 092319

1) Vision. Transition from event-primary communication to vision/strategy-primary communication with redirected and more effective wins for congregation and ministries.

2) Outline.

- What: 1) Develop categories, definitions and tool to support vision/strategy-level communication plan for each 6-month ministry horizon; 2) create buy-in and use at MinLdr, Ministry Staff, and key volunteer levels.

- How: Vet and refine proposed StratComm Grid tool

- When: October 2019; ready for use in Nov 2019 sequencing

- Whom: MinLdrs, Ministry Staff, and key volunteer leaders

- How much (minimum 2 budget/resource approaches—ie: A. no/low budget, B. park avenue): $0.00

3) Hurdles. As best you can see at the moment.

- Agreement regarding levels of priority

- A strong enough redirected yes

- Agreement on refined capacities (both weekly and in each comm channel)

4) Circle 1. Who should be in first round of vetting/refinement?

- MH/DAS, DH, MinLdrs, Ministry Staff, Key volunteers (need to be identified by MinLdrs)

****

That's it. All you need to start is a good run at v1.

Sometimes I think we over-complicate this whole issue in wanting (or feeling the pressure to get) everything down on paper before even starting the conversation. That will ensure project-stall like nothing else.

Get a sketch down. Write up a v1.

> Phase 1: concept to vetting,

> Version 1: basic ideas and hopes,

> Circle 1: a core workgroup caring about the outcomes and willing to join the fun.

Phase 2—vetting to plan

A workable and effective path forward on all aspects of the project. Budget. Personnel. Deliverables. Timeline.

In this phase...

The workgroup expands to any additional voices (Circle 2), especially those directly impacted by project outcomes. This group work produces a v2: a refined roadmap including all expected project research and tasks. It asks whether the project might enjoy another circle of voices (Circle 3), this time looking for those with an indirect connection to the project outcomes but a sphere of influence or experience related to the project, ie—interested professionals in your congregation or community.

Which leads to...

Phase 3—plan to implementation

Movement toward timely launch, implementation or completion, and...

Phase 4—elebration and future adjustments

No project should leave this step undone, but it's often the most challenging of the phases. It's surprisingly difficult to both aptly appreciate hard work while simultaneously keeping an eye on what could go better in the future. Both are critical. Good leaders find a way to keep both in play. I will freely admit this is the hardest phase for me personally.

So, back up and out of the weeds for a second. You'll note we've tried to account for:

- a common rhythm—encouraging ministry-wide expectations and process. *What ever happened to that project? Oh, it's still in phase 2 at the moment.*

- enough process—allowing for appropriate refinement and approach.

- a right representation of voices leading to a decision to proceed, when, and how.

Knowable. Repeatable. Invisible. Scalable.

Vision folks will love phase one and feel like checking out in phases 1-3. Logistics hound dogs will snarl at first but pretty quickly light up. The entire team will appreciate phase 4 celebration while struggling with future adjustments. Your job is to keep everyone moving forward with the end result front and center and enough structural direction to light the way.

Does this resemble the way in which your teams and leaders envision and collaborate around important things? If not, let's take some ground and make things better for everyone. Like all new tools, adopting a more standardized approach to projects takes practice and a commitment to some measure of change. But even a full 4 phase, 3 version, 3 circle project$_9$ can zoom right along. It's all in the scope and pace of those phases. And the huge, gnarly projects? It produces enough check and conversation to assure we didn't miss anything... or anyone.

For another real-world project using this structure see Appendix A.

For extra credit, and an extra measure of precision, I am including an additional tool in the end-matter known as a Logical Framework, largely borrowed from international project management expert Terry Schmidt. Becoming conversant with it will only increase confidence and buy-in among church staff and key volunteer leaders.

Let's be patient with ourselves and others, generous in conversation and inclusion while traversing the phases. Soon you'll feel a growing predictability to the whole thing. Trust and collaboration will be healthier and deeper.

And ministry may just begin to flow a little better.

Eve

It had been on her mind for awhile.
Maybe better just to say it outloud.

 "Right. No. It didn't get in the announcements. Again."

She paused.

"Why can't you guys get your act together?"

The phone came down hard in its base. For weeks she had been emailing and calling the mission partner. Given their travel schedule, the task was daunting. This coming Tuesday was all that was possible. It had to be in front of everyone on Sunday or what was the point?

If people could just see what she'd seen on her field visit. Push everything else. God was on the move. His people needed to know it.

Another God-moment squandered.

Maybe this church didn't really care about the great commission after all.

Planning Rhythms:
Piranha or Grouper?

They say where there's blood in the water...

We don't mean to. Honestly. But church staff are so passionate about the Lord's work that we tend to carry a few (understandable) blind spots. Especially so, if a staff is more or less constituted as a group of para-church ministry leaders. Our needs seemed reasonable. They probably were. Then again, it's hard to tell without taking another step.

Recently I visited some larger churches in the Minneapolis area to ask questions of their tech, communications, and operations staff. I wanted to get a sense of their scope of ministry and any tools or approaches they were finding effective. One conversation included a church's count of "events" on their church calendar in a ministry year. This is a church of over 10,000 and they were counting every service, gathering, and ministry item that needed scheduling. Makes sense, as once it's on the schedule it has to be managed, adjusted, and communicated. Somewhere in the neighborhood of 5000 "events" landed on their calendar. I immediately wondered about our church. Geeky, yes, but I couldn't wait to get back and do a count.

4500.

For a church of 1300.

Yikes.

Digging a little deeper I saw a ministry planning environment that in my mind was neither sustainable nor scalable. Both critical goals, wouldn't you say? From that vantage point I observed two major planning aims for our church.

1) Move from an always on-always open environment to an agreed-upon and workable ministry horizon.

2) Quantify capacities in order to thrive within our capacities.

Ministry Horizon

The first big move is transitioning from an always on-always open environment to an agreed-upon rhythm in which a significant ministry horizon will be largely, if not completely, locked and loaded. Plan the work together for a significant period. No additions. I get how restrictive this sounds but I guarantee, it can be done and not bring everything good, creative, and Spirit-responsive to a shuddering halt. Before you dismiss the idea out of hand, please note:

- the time horizon needs to be long enough to create a sense of direction and planning but not so big that you can't actually foresee what the Lord may ask you to go after.

- you are not attempting to plan every breath, meeting, and project of your staff, only the events and initiatives requiring direct use of your three, key capacities: operations (space/maintenance), tech (AV equipment and qualified operators), and communication (all available channels).

- there are ways to plan well and stay responsive. It's called margin and is directly related to the section below (capacities).

Without a workable ministry horizon, we end up with sharks in the water. Well-meaning sharks, but still very sharky. The staff with the most dependable ministry schedule or who's the most savvy with these kinds of things will get to the calendar chumball first. Everyone else gets what's left. Those last into the water will scratch their heads, even as their stomachs growl at the meager offerings settling to the bottom.

As much as I am for natural consequences, this is not a good way to dole out ministry resources. Sure, it's a knowable system. Kind of. How far out front can someone make a request? The next five years? Twelve months? Oh, and they have to bring their requests at a point in the year that makes sense for everyone?

Sounds like you're advocating for a ministry horizon. You're just not making it very strategic on the whole.

Please, give this some thought. Because here is the absolutely beautiful upside: this may just be how the huge, all-ministry endeavors become truly the huge, all-ministry endeavors. Lead Pastors, cry hallelujah. Does it often feel that the 30,000 foot level vision ends up being shoe-horned with every last event and gathering? Maybe it's time to do something a little different.

> **"Without a workable ministry horizon, we end up with sharks in the water. Well-meaning sharks, but still very sharky."**

Which leads to our second aim.

Capacities

Quantifying your capacities in the three key areas helps you work hard, but within... your capacities. One of the direct outcomes of such a rhythm is an easier way to say, for example: "Oh, week 2 is full up on communication channels. We'll need to reschedule some of these requests. When might that work?" We've all experienced it. No rhythms = no real way to see when we're breaking the bank, aside from people feeling (esp. in the case of communication) that a million messages just came at them yet not a single one rose to its desired impact.

But this also helps you decide whether you want to purposefully leave margin for those initiatives you pray will surface. Are you a ministry that likes to run at 100%? Ok, you can't be a very responsive ministry. How about setting aside 20% of your quantified capacities for the excitement of the unexpected? You just have to become comfortable with running at 80% during "normal" ministry time. It shouldn't need calling out, but you can't really do both (run at 100% and turn on a dime)—either very well or for very long. Does this sound like your experience?

I recently heard a pastor talk about "downtime" after a heavy season. In theory, this could be a helpful ministry horizon idea. What I'd be very curious to hear is whether the staff really felt this was a livable rhythm (and whether it actually filters down to everyone's experience or just a few), or just the pastor's good attempt to identify and address the reality of ministry pushes. And, very importantly, whether those ministry pushes tend to come out of nowhere or from within the context of an established and understood ministry horizon.

We often utilize in ministry a rhythm no sane business leader would employ. Just try porting it over to this kind of environment and see what happens. One day you're happily throwing Widget A into the machine, thinking you can get the order done on time for Tuesday's delivery. What are those new boxes?

Oh, that's just Widget B. It uses the same machine and is due on Wednesday. By the way, Widget B takes four days to prep and produce. What do you do? You work harder. And you try to work smarter. But as Widgets C, D, and E all make their presence known on the production floor (with no prior announcement), you can only do so much. And that's only the production side of the equation. When the CFO sees a massive uptick in unexpected overtime, he's got to figure out how to tell his boss and the board. Profit margin suffers. Investors get edgy about putting more resources into a business that seems a bit chaotic, unpredictable.

Let's just say it: people are more important than widgets and ministry is not a venture to be invested in only on the promise of a good quarterly report.

Let's look at a planning rhythm heading in a healthier direction.

Planning Rhythms:
A Suggested Approach

2 horizons. 3 phases. 1 close and open.

 This ain't your grandpa's church calendar. And, by the way, how do items get on the church calendar? Easy. Church Secretary. Lesson: be nice to your church secretary.

But that's the old school method. What we're talking about here is a shiny, new Calendar 2.0. Maybe even a 3.0.

We're aiming to move forward on two fronts:

1) from basic organization (good) to something that facilitates strategic value (great), while

2) significantly shifting from individual planning (good) to strategy-leader combined efforts (great).

With a Cal 1.0 there's good forethought from single leaders who look for ministry dates when they're ready enough to try and lock things in. If they're super early, they likely get everything they wanted. If not, they either adjust their dates or scuttle their vision.

Neither is a healthy outcome.

With a Cal 2.0 a leadership team moves into a process where a rhythm is engaged and expectations are set for when the calendar will be filled out, or—in our language—sequenced. A general awareness grows regarding the scope of ministry across staff and key volunteer leadership. This is good. It can also be quite unsettling. While broader understanding and a more reliable rhythm is achieved, the general posture is still a "yes to all" that comes forward.

In a Cal 3.0, leadership applies filters to the three key capacities and a process that works from a strategic viewpoint, not merely the support of ministry events. More active and diverse churches will find this step to be quite hard. It also holds the greatest potential gains.

Take a moment and place yourself on this spectrum.

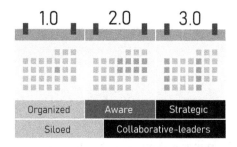

Can you imagine the benefits of moving from 1.0 to 2.0? 2.0 to 3.0? Refining what may be an already very collaborative team into a more strategic unit? I'll assume all of us have some experience with a Calendar 1.0. Moving to Cal 2.0 is not a difficult structure, but it is a very significant measure of change. For our purposes, I am using two ministry horizons of 6mos each.

How to build it

Divide the year into (2) 6mos Ministry Horizons. We'll call them MinHorizA (Jan-Jun) and MinHorizB (Jul-Dec).

Each Ministry Horizon comprises:

> Four months of prayer and planning and two months of what we'll call sequencing—the point where everyone brings their good planning to the staff table. It normally takes the form of two all-team meetings with follow-up work as needed.

Now we have:

- MinHorizA (Jan-Apr prayer/planning, May-Jun sequencing) and

• MinHorizB (Jul-Oct prayer/planning, Nov-Dec sequencing).

Four months of development and two months of sequencing lead to six months of implementation. How about a visual before we go too much further:

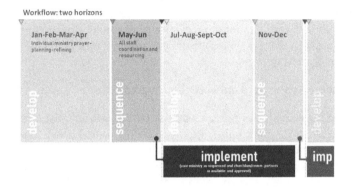

• Four months of prayer and planning.

• Two months of sequencing.

• Six months of implementation.

Next, establish an open and closed door for two categories of ministry: core ministry and church family/community partners. What are these two categories?

Core ministry falls under the purview of ministry staff or key volunteer leaders and is generally associated with your stated strategies. For instance, our church strategies are gather (in worship), connect (in a small group), and serve (home, church, community, world). The vast majority of what we need to calendar logically falls under those headings.

Church family means events hosted by those who consider you their home church but not related directly to your church strategies or ministry departments. Birthday parties, receptions, showers, graduation celebrations. You get the idea. You also may have some measure of community groups using your spaces and resources. These would be **community partners**. A few of ours are the county veterans board, United Way, and a summer day camp for kids on the autism spectrum.

Here's the action-step: close the core ministry door in order to open the church family/community partner door. And, in reverse: don't open the door for churchfam-community partners until you've closed the door for core ministry.

We are literally saying we will add no more core ministry events or initiatives during the succeeding implementation phase (after closing). Per our visual above, once the May sequencing meetings have happened, we work the plan for July-December, unaltered. We are also saying we will consider no church family/community partner requests for that same period (July-December) until finalizing core ministry sequencing in May.

Please let the gains here outweigh your skepticism.

To move from an always-open always-on paradigm you must stop taking requests at some point (albeit gently and only temporarily). When you bring the entire staff together for a 6mos plan you establish the resources spoken for over the next 6mos. Only then will you know your *yes* to church family and community partner requests. Correct, this is a de facto establishment of core ministry needs as priority number one. And again: if you decide on a paradigm of something less than 100% capacity in order to remain more responsive as a ministry, you will be sequencing something less than 100% of those capacities. That's likely an easier pill to swallow but requires far greater discipline to maintain the margin.

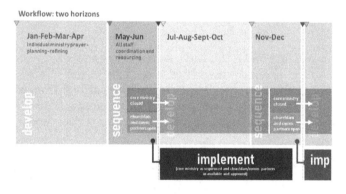

Okay. Here's the visual with the open/close factor:

After all your hard work you have a plan for the next 6mos that can be described as:

- core ministry: sequenced and resourced, and

- churchfam/commpartners: open and subject to availability.

Simple structure. Knowable. Repeatable. Invisible. Scalable. And all the confidence you need to move ahead as one.

> **"To move from an always-open always-on paradigm you must stop taking requests at some point (albeit gently and only temporarily)."**

So, how do the details get in place? Great question. The outline so far is really just a tool to bring it all together at the highest level. Here's a basic 30 day run-up, and steps following, the sequencing sessions:

- 30 days before sequencing: submissions open and Cal 2 draft built

- Sequencing Session 1: Make sure all submissions made it accurately onto Cal 2 tool

- 30 day interim: build out requested capacities in operations, tech, and communication

- Sequencing Session 2: staff review assigned capacities and 1) accept and move toward event or 2) schedule event consult to discuss and refine assigned capacities and plans.

- Ministry Horizon begins with some event consults ongoing (usually scheduled -60 days from event or program start date)

A quick word on event consults

Your staff will initially bristle at the thought (What? Another meeting?). Especially if they manage a multitude of programs and events. But here's the question to probe: they will absolutely be getting the details together at some point. An event consult covers everything they'll need... and more... in one sitting... without the confusion of an email string.

The goal is to get them feeling like your support ministry team is an active partner, giving best-practices consult, and in a timely and strategic fashion. That only happens if we take some of the diversity of approach out of the planning equation. A standardized consult will do that and help all involved feel like a team. Because now, they actually are. For a visual of our current outline for event consults, see Appendix B.

Ministry leaders will soon find they don't have to carry alone the nebulous weight of details. Support Team members will love being in on the goals and needs of the ministry vision, and in a fashion resembling that of all the other ministry leaders.

Win-win.

The Questions I Always Get (in preemptive answer format)

Yes, some kind of form or tool (your version of a Calendar 2.0 or 3.0) is necessary for the sequencing sessions and resulting plan. On the simple side, an excel sheet organized as a "modified" waterfall works great. On the complex end, a piece of software like Asana will do the job fantastically. I've added examples of both in the end-matter.

Yes, sequencing sessions prep comes from every staff member with an event or initiative requiring resourcing from any of the three key capacities. A simple form works fine and generally two weeks before the first sequencing session, allowing the sequencing leader time to develop a first draft of the ministry plan.

No, there are rarely contests of strength or wit to untangle ministry requests asking for competing resources. The working presumption is that you can make about 90% of the requests happen as requested or strategically envisioned. About 10% may need a rescheduling or change. You will need to predetermine who holds veto power and how it will be applied in those rare instances.

A key post-sequencing step is establishing a weekly tag for the three key capacities in question. Remember, you're going to open the door for church family and community partner requests next, so you need to know what's available and possible. Something like:

Green = looks good; Orange = probably, but more complex options may not be available; Red = yeah, that's funny no we'll all die

This last question I'll frame in a statement, as it's often posed that way.

"I'm concerned there's no room for flexibility here. You know, ministry life is not an assembly line."

True. Did I mention we're only sequencing work requiring operations, tech, or communication resources?

You want to have a meeting of area youth pastors. You'll set up the room. You'll reset it the way you found it. I have trained you on using your laptop with the big tv. The broader church doesn't need to know about this via Sunday announcements, social media, email, or cans with wire string. And you thought of it just now? Awesome. The room is open. Enjoy.

"You mean you don't care?"

No, we don't care. At least regarding our planning rhythms and capacities. No capacities affected? No problem. This should provide some measure of comfort for the more improvisational among us.

But... the second you ask for something with room setup and a spot in the announcements video—and we've already locked up our ministry horizon plan—you'll get shot down faster than a MAGA balloon over Nancy Pelosi's house.

Yes, a fair amount of flexibility is pre-built into the system. And yes, there are understandable exceptions. Best practice? Make sure exceptions are exceptional. Here are a few we've encountered.

- Weddings/Funerals—Weddings regularly require more than the 6mos window to plan. Consider whether a cap on their frequency is helpful if you are being overrun in this category. Funerals are one way we want to respond quickly and lovingly. This is just us being Jesus' people at a time of folk's greatest pain and need.

- Mission Partner visits—Surprise. We're here. The shorter end of the time spectrum as well.

- Retreat or event speaker or band that requires more than 6mos advance booking—No one wants their event held hostage by the 6mos rule. Probably best to bend it at the point they get a contract signed. Or just go after that 80s Christian Metal band making the rounds on the casino circuit. I hear they've got some free dates this year.

Okay, but what about the jump from Cal 2.0 to 3.0?

Easy to summarize, challenging to implement, huge payoff. You will no longer take every event submission in with the understanding that everything is a yes, or at least a yes to the exact desired plan as submitted for the three key capacities. Instead, strategy leaders establish a hierarchy of initiatives and dates occupying the three key capacities before the first sequencing session.

It's your basic big rocks before little rocks approach. Both are important, but you can't really build a wall by starting with the smaller pieces. And yes, you are now establishing there are in fact some pieces to your ministry wall that are centrally strategic for the whole and others that are some degree less.

Again, not unimportant, but think of a tree with a hundred branches. Sometimes the branches can get all the attention while the trunk suffers. At some point, event-busy churches find their most important church-wide messaging and efforts being lost in the fray of a hundred other, good things. It's not their fault, necessarily. But they have staffed, resourced, and reinforced this kind of approach. Extremely patient and committed leadership will be required to move toward something more strategic.

> **"At some point, event-busy churches find their most important church-wide messaging and efforts being lost in the fray of a hundred other, good things."**

A Cal 3.0 is the exact opposite of a Cal 1.0 in this respect. In the old system, the early bird got fat. Now, being early only means you're handing off your submissions to the strategy team before everyone else. Okay-- rocks, walls, trees, birds. Going back to our original metaphor: the sharks are now all waiting to see what's "left over." But they're doing it together. In love. On mission. Strategically.

For more Planning Rhythms visuals, please see Appendix B.

Ben

He couldn't believe he'd missed that.

But then again...

 He scanned the notes. Sure enough. Buried in the pile, on a green sticky.

"45 chrs. 8 roundtbls. Pdm. Othr rms need lng tbls w/no chr. Unlck only west. Bbq no cols."

It seemed correct at the time. Now, he wasn't so sure.

And Pastor was pretty upset.

It's not every day you host fifty other church leaders.

He'd tried to ask some questions. Pastor was on the run, as usual.

Now he just felt bad.

Resource Use:
No Custom Pizzas Over the Phone

... but, how about this?

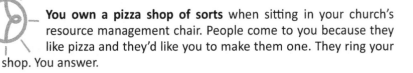 **You own a pizza shop of sorts** when sitting in your church's resource management chair. People come to you because they like pizza and they'd like you to make them one. They ring your shop. You answer.

"Hello."

"Uh, yeah. I got your number and I'd like to order a pizza. Do you have a website with a menu or can you read me some options?"

"Oh, no. No menu. Just tell me what you want."

They rattle off a list of ingredients and then stop. "Excuse me, are you writing this down?"

"Nope," pointing to your old noggin. "Got it all up here. We're good."

You say goodbye, heading to the wood-fired ovens in back. Twenty minutes later a piping hot pie comes out, set on the counter.

The phone rings again.

"Hello."

"Uh, yeah. Me again. Is my pizza ready?"

"Sure is."

"Were you going to call me? Or should I just come on in?"

"Either way is fine by me."

Customer, arriving ten minutes later: "Hey, what's up with the little bread chunks?"

"Well, that's what you asked for. I thought it was a little weird but you know... "

Palm to forehead. "I asked if you took coupons... not if I could have croutons."

Custom is cool—until it's impractical

But here's the challenge: church feels like we should be able to do custom because it seems more personal. You know, people are diverse so meet people's needs in all their multiplicity.

If we're talking about counseling, prayer, or leading a small group, fine, let's be as aware of and intentional about meeting people's diverse needs as we can. We're not talking about that list. We're talking about rooms, tables, chairs, web events, announcements, and projectors. You can't add enough staffing to offer a concierge experience for each person wanting these resources.

You've tried. You know what I mean. At some point, everyone is served better with a menu. And one of the primary aspects of a menu is naming things.

So, what's in a name? Clarity. Dependability. A sense of calm, even when lots of pizzas are flying in and out of the ovens. You know what they are, who they're going to, and how to do them really, really well. Here's a short list of the gains we gain experience from simply beginning to organize our resources around categories and options.

1. A menu based on the mission of the church instead of the multiplicity of people's desires.

> We want to serve people. And their desires are not evil. But, again, the endless complexities of people need not translate to endlessly complex systems and resources in the church. Smaller churches may get away with this for a while. Growth and complexity are not your friends when using this model. And

(perhaps?) you serve people best by offering consistently what you do best.

2. Clarity about the "order."

What's up next? Oh, a #2 pepperoni and black olive.

3. Handy assessment of capacities based on categories and usage—the resources you purchase or keep on hand.

How many cans of black olives to stock? If all is custom: hard to tell. If the #2 is a customer fav and top seller, you can gauge how much shelf space to give to the little black beauties. Yes, I like olives.

4. A better way to gently decline and redirect.

With no menu you are faced with the "I know you have the ingredients. Why can't you make me a peanut butter and pickle pizza?" For one, because that's gross, but also, no—we've taken time to figure out what it is we do really well here and we'd like to see if one of those options can work for you.

So, move toward some basic offerings. That's step one and we'll go into the details in the suggested approach chapter to follow. But there was also a mass of confusion around two other elements in our pizza shop example.

Did you notice that the order was taken verbally? A bit of a stretch when it comes to church resources, right? I mean, you would never promise something to someone without writing it down... right? But the real problem is not so much verbal transfer of needs versus paper and pen. The more likely challenge is formal versus informal.

An informal resource requests system provides no reference mechanism, in case of an error or misunderstanding. It also lacks a way to actually close the conversation and confirm the resulting resource approval.

In short, a breeding ground for confusion, dropped balls, and completely unnecessary tensions and conflicts.

No thanks.

Three phases (intake, approval, confirmation) will be needed in a more formalized approach to church resource use. So, what kind of systems or tools can help? Frankly, the choices are almost too many these days. Desktop and web-based solutions abound. Most have (generally) the same bells and vary on whistles.

Here's the issue: without macro systems to guide, they merely manage the flurry of custom-order pizzas at the micro-level by organizing the particular components of a custom order. While bringing a measure of assistance with gains 2 and 3 listed above, they miss on the others and may only dig us a deeper hole—filled with custom order pizzas.

A custom church resource shop is problematic. Another, better path exists.

The alternative? Name things. And then use a formalized intake, approval, and confirmation system with those named things.

As before, we'll shape this "menu" around our key capacities:

- Room capacities (groupings of room sizes/uses) and operational staffing (ops team setup/reset)

- Tech/AV (range of AV options and staffing)

- Communication Channels (print, live, video, web, email)

Resources Use:
A Suggested Approach

Use-Matrix. Capacities. Confirmation.

 Okay, ready to take orders based on a new menu? Nope. We haven't yet created the thing. And even when we do, we won't show it to anyone.

Surprise. The menu is for internal organization only. Hang with me a moment and all will be revealed. This approach requires categorization work, yes, but then we'll use our menu (of categories) without putting it in front of anyone. And then we'll confirm what item(s) they ordered.

Without them knowing they ordered from the menu.

Sadly, we are not making pizzas. We're dealing with rooms, chairs, tables, lights, sound, staging, lecterns, wipe-off boards, kitchens, gyms, emails, church announcements, web events...

No one wants to see a menu of those things. Still, we absolutely need one. A secret menu if you will.

Step One—Develop a Use-Matrix

A matrix is an organizational tool that sorts elements by various factors and then reveals the possible combinations of those factors. In our particular case, a matrix helps us determine the interplay of room size, operational support, and AV needs. For communication, it helps us think through intended audience and placement into and frequency of various communication tools or channels.

Let's hit the ops and tech side of things first. So, a simple question: are there some obvious size "fits" for your church spaces? We found three at our church:

<50   50-150   >150

Next, let's ask whether the use requires operational setup/tear down. Two factors address the likely operational staffing needs. We might call them:

User-set (US) or Operational-set (OS)

Last, we'll want to consider any audio-visual needs. Three options surface:

Basic—no AV needs or simple connection from laptop or tablet to large tv

AV1—more complex visual needs and a few microphones or audio sources

AV2—anything more complex than AV1

Fantastic. You now have a room size, operations staffing, and AV matrix. A menu. Options from which to choose and direct people into appropriate scenarios.

Here's what it looks like:

	US			OS		
	Basic	AV1	AV2	Basic	AV1	AV2
<50	<50 USB	<50 USA1	<50 USA2	<50 OSB	<50 OSA1	<50 OSA2
50-150	50-150 USB	50-150 USA1	50-150 USA2	50-150 OSB	50-150 OSA1	50-150 OSA2
>150	>150 USB	>150 USA1	>150 USA2	>150 OSB	>150 OSA1	>150 OSA2

18 Items (the white boxes) on the menu. And we may not even have eighteen options. Let's go real-world for a moment. Pick a few of the menu items and match a probable use case to them.

For example: >150USB. Think this through for a second. More than 150 people with absolutely no audio-visual needs are using only what is already in the room and will reset it when finished. Can you imagine a common use-case? You make the call on whether it vanishes from the menu or you leave it with some further conditional-use tag. Either way, it pays to see what might be eliminated right out of the gate.

Alright, how about communication? Much the same process but with different questions. Our use-matrix here involves three factors as well: strategic value, call to action, and audience.

- Strategic value ("How does this foster our stated purposes as a church?") has three levels: 1) mission critical (must), 2) mission strategic (should), 3) mission enhancing (can).

- Call to action ("What response are we asking of our people?") has largely two flavors: 1) do (act, grow, become), 2) go (attend, join, participate).

- Audience ("How many people are you trying to move to this action?") falls into three likely sizes: 1) 100% (all), 50% (half), and 30% (some).

It looks like this:

	Do (act, grow, become)			Go (attend, join, participate)		
	100%	50%	30%	100%	50%	30%
Critical	all must do	half must do	some must do	all must go	half must go	some must go
Strategic	all should do	half should do	some should do	all should go	half should go	some should go
Enhance	all can do	half can do	some can do	all can go	half can go	some can go

Services Announcements, Print | Social | Web Promo, All-Church Email

Print | Social | Web Promo, All-Church Email

Groups Announcements, Ministry | Department Email, Person-Person

The additional piece here is to define three communication channels and the tools best suited to a particular communication initiative. In our matrix, red= tier one and includes service announcements, print | social | web promotion, and all church email. Yellow= tier two and utilizes print | social | web promos and all-church email. Blue= tier 3 and relies upon announcements in groups, ministry | department hosted email, and person to person promo. These are general guidelines, as your particular channels may vary.

Granted, the communication matrix only points you in the right direction, requiring some hard conversations about where to put what. The size of a room is a defined constant. Someone's perception of their ministry as "must-do" is a whole other deal. But then again, you'd be surprised how open-minded folks can be when given some filters. Mostly they want to know 1) there is a process, and 2) the process is reasonable, transparent, and dependable.

Or, as we like to say of macro-systems in general, knowable, repeatable, and scalable.

So far we've done some great work in reducing operations, tech, and communication requests from "it feels infinite" to something more manageable. But let's not get too excited. No one wants to see this. The images above only serve as unnecessary complication for the end-user: a code no one wants to learn. Instead, we've got to get them using the matrix without knowing they're using the matrix.

Hold it, didn't you just say transparency was one of the key concerns for people accessing church resources? Yep. And there may be a point at which you go behind the counter and show someone how the sausage is made. But remember, most people don't actually think this way. It's very difficult to place a chart in front of them and have them immediately see the value and wisdom in it. You'll need to translate.

And that's again why we want to take our next step.

Step Two—Provide qualifying questions to locate their request in the matrix.

Here's how this will go down. First, for operations and tech.

4 qualifying questions.

> Q1: Will your event need more than 1 main space?
>
> options: yes | no
>
> Q2: How many people do you expect (at any one time)?
>
> options: less than 50 | 50-150 | more than 150
>
> Q3: Will you require operational setup or tear down?

options: yes | no

Q4: Will you require audio-visual equipment or support?

options: no av or yes—a simple laptop to large tv connection | yes—a few microphones and/or audio inputs and visual support | yes—we have more complex needs than that

"... most people don't actually think this way. It's very difficult to place a chart in front of them and have them immediately see the value and wisdom in it. You'll need to translate."

Surprise. We placed them into the operations and tech matrix. With one caveat. Our matrix only deals with single room use requests. A yes to question 1 sends them to the head of the line for a resource-use consult. The first question—do you need more than one room—triages the requests and sends complexity to a place where it can be handled well.

So, let's look again at real-world. Single room real-world.

Q1=50-150

Q2=yes

Q3=no

Turns out what they need is a 50-150 OSB. It was a youth pizza party with a laptop playing background videos on a large tv.

Awesome. Do we do that?

Okay, now over to communication. Here's our qualifying questions:

Q1: Are you calling people to "do" something (act, grow, become) or "go" to (attend, join, participate) something?

options: do | go

Q2: How many people are you calling to respond?

options: 100% of congregation | 50% of congregation | 30% or less of congregation

Q3: How important is your request to the overall stated mission of the church?

options: critical (without it, we will fail) | strategic (without it, we will falter) | enhancement (without it, we will fade)

Okay, they answered: go, 50%, strategic. Turns out it was a men's retreat.

How many Men's Retreats have you communicated on Sunday morning in front of everyone? The Men's Ministry may not like to hear this but that's bad placement for their request. But it's not even really that we "placed" a communication asset badly. Of greater concern is that there may have been a true "do, 100%, critical" that either didn't get recognized as such or it had to be shoe-horned in with items of lesser urgency and missional value.

Communication is a capacity.

We only have so many tools and moments to do it with/in and people only have so many items they can process and receive in a manner that leads them to action. Recently our children's director reminded me of this with a quote from the "immortal Dashiell Parr" of the Pixar animated franchise, "The Incredibles." In reply to his mom's assertion that everyone is special, he opined:

"That just means no one is special."

Dash is one smart dude.

Step 3—Allow the Use Matrix to suggest a ranked set of options

Your intake system will receive the qualifying questions, label the request by name (ex:—50-150 OSB) and then present the internal scheduler with a ranked list of possibilities. Ours sends me a nice little email that says, "Hey, someone has asked for a 50-150 OSB on X date at Y time. Here are some options: Room A, Room B, Room F, Room J."

Bravo, we've cut the possibilities and known next steps considerably. How much? If Room A is actually available on X date at Y time and no intervening factors exist (see workflow step below)... 5 minutes or less.

On the communication side of things it's a similar process. Qualifying questions lead to a comm channel assignment, which in turn has a pre-defined set of comm tools and their frequencies. The Men's Retreat mentioned above was a "go,50%,strategic." That's a tier 2 channel with print | web | social promos and all-church email. Here's an important caveat: with communications you may end up adding tools from the tier below (in this case maybe ministry | department email from the Men's

Ministry to their mailing list), but you are never accessing tools from the tier above.

Step 4—Create a closed loop

Let's make sure we finish in a way that provides confidence for both process and outcome. Ideally, any kind of follow-up should be:

1) Standardized and easily retrievable. Ad Hoc email confirmation, voicemail, or text is frankly not our best effort. A well-designed confirmation email from a custom database or online form system is better-practice.

2) Detailed to the degree that times, dates, details, setups, room locations, fees, comm tools and dates, etc are all near-impossible to misinterpret for the end-user.

3) Inviting further engagement as needed.

This kind of reply creates a sense of the support team's joyful collaboration as opposed to miserly distribution of the fruits of their realm.

Last up.

Step 5—Design a workflow

Steps 1-4 get us a system (more visuals and examples in end matter). We also need to know how people and requests will go from start to finish. This will be quick and generic but should give you the needed steps to design a workflow specific to your church.

First contact: direct a phone call, email, or in-person request to the intake tool (paper or electronic). DO NOT take a detailed memo. Get them to the qualifying questions as quickly as possible.

System Triage: Either 1) Initial thank you and "we're getting right to work on your request" reply that mirrors everything they put down on the intake tool (confidence point 1 is gained when they see you got everything they needed you to get), or 2) redirect to resource-use consult as soon as scheduling allows.

Internal: 1) matrix notifies scheduler of request and approved use options, 2) scheduler checks for availability and tags request as moving forward or waiting on intervening issues (ie—fees deposit required before formal scheduling), 3) internal vetting/approvals as needed by other team members (ie—tech, ops, comm), 4) request completed and formally scheduled.

Confirmation: Requester receives a well-designed reply with all details and easy channels of follow-up.

Great job.

While system design work can be satisfying, the point is not so much to create a well-oiled machine as to make sure the machine is well-oiled. Your church has resources to support life-changing ministry. Why in the world would we want to make accessing those resources difficult or chaotic?

Spend time here. Then watch it flow.

Next Steps

Thanks so much for the time and attention.

 I do hope it's been a help.

And maybe a little fun.

Let's finish where we began.

... the image of your church staff and key leaders as a circuit of energy, an electrical current that flows freely to do the "job" of the Gospel. When working correctly, it's easy to spot. The Word: informing and shaping interactions. The joyful Family of God living out its calling. The presence, gifts, and fruit of the Spirit—on full display and being put to use. Reconciliation and grace in misunderstandings. Hope and energy towards a collective future. Transformation.

So, do effective church systems create this much-desired free flow of the Gospel in and through us?

Heavens, no.

They merely give us a shot at engaging the hard work of relationships, ideas, and programming for which we are gifted and trained. Good systems: get at it. Bad systems: we keep coming back to the fact that something's working against us unnecessarily.

Here's to fixing what we can and persevering in love through the rest, working towards the day when our staff and key volunteer leaders can regularly breathe and think.

Imagine the good flowing from that.

I would be so glad to hear of the gains and equally glad to be involved at any step along the way.

In Jesus,

wayne.stewart@waynecstewart.com

Sign up for the ChurchFlow newsletter and receive Support Ministry case-studies, tips, software reviews, and more.

Subscribe to the churchflow podcast at churchflow.org—coming March 2020.

Thanks

To David Staff and Mark Henderson, for the kind of senior leadership required to even begin to address these issues and the grace to work them out over time.

To Jeremy Bents, Derek Hanson, Jonathan Anderson, and Andrew Swanson for being an amazing lab crew for these ideas and the willingness to believe they might make a difference.

To the broader staff and congregation of Christ Community Church for allowing some admittedly out of the box approaches and displaying a great desire for impact in unity, time and again.

Appendix A

Real-World PM

At the risk of getting too "meta", here's the documents and images from our church's journey to implementing a new planning rhythm (yes, the plan to develop a planning rhythm :)

Image 1 is the basic v1 we talked about in Chapter 2:

Christ Community Church
Process and Project Worksheet V1

Process/Project Title: CCC ministry workflow
Initiated by/date: WCS 060418 *see also logframe attached to Asana project*
General format: one page, more bullets than paragraphs.

1) Vision. *What gain(s) will be celebrated when we accomplish this thing?*

> *Position CCC for even greater Spirit-empowered impact (esp. 10yr/Vision 15k)... leading to connecting people to life-defining relationships in Christ.*

2) Outline. *Broad sketch needing input through vetting circles; time spent developing should represent both general nature but also any known, pre-established non-negotiables.*

> What: *foster innovation while practicing good teamsmanship*
>
> How: *design/implement workflow system that manages all initiatives and requests via agreed upon cycles of ideation, vetting, and execution.*
>
> When: *circles 1 and 2 August; greenlight v3 by 081518; orientation/training Aug 21; full implementation at Jan 2019 ministry horizon.*
>
> Whom: *all staff, primarily run through ministry leads, fac sched workgroup, and SMin.*
>
> How much (minimum 2 budget/resource approaches—ie: A. no/low budget, B. park avenue): *A. no budget—systems and gauges, training materials and visuals produced in-house; B. $5-10k for systems and gauges development by contracted firm.*

3) Hurdles. *As best you can see at the moment.* Put these in question form--no more than three.

- *Buy-in and practice from all staff as the new way we serve together?*
- *How to limit/manage exceptions so the rhythm works for everyone?*
- *Can we design/implement data management systems that truly give order and live/accurate feedback?*

4) Circle 1. *Who should be in first round of vetting/refinement?*
> *Pre-v1 conversations (before 6/18): MH, SMin team, Fac Sched workgroup.*
> *Circle 1/v1=DAS, MH; Circle 2=Min Ldrs group.*

Image 2 is the outline of the project in our project management software, Asana:

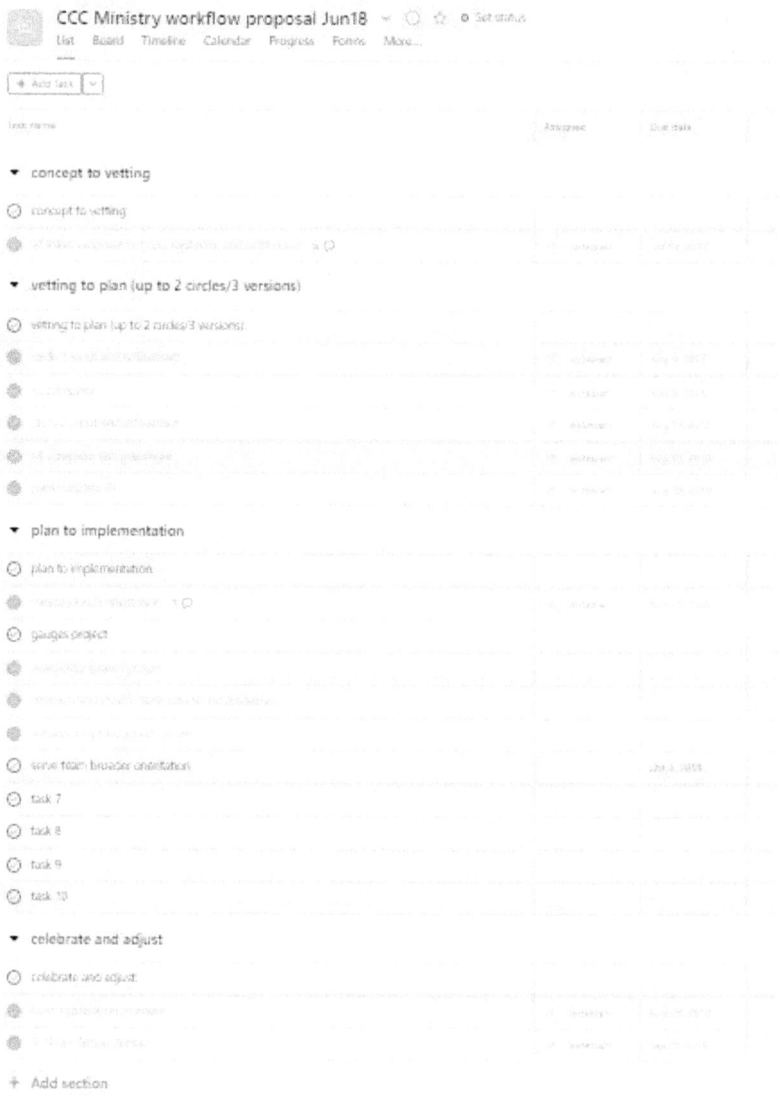

CCC Ministry workflow proposal Jun18

List Board Timeline Calendar Progress Forms More...

+ Add task

Task name   Assignee   Due date

▼ concept to vetting

○ concept to vetting

● ...

▼ vetting to plan (up to 2 circles/3 versions)

○ vetting to plan (up to 2 circles/3 versions)

●

●

●

●

●

▼ plan to implementation

○ plan to implementation

●

○ gauges project

●

●

●

○ serve team broader orientation

○ task 7

○ task 8

○ task 9

○ task 10

▼ celebrate and adjust

○ celebrate and adjust

●

●

+ Add section

Image 3 is the bonus Logical Framework piece:

CCC Ministry Workflow

	Objectives	Success Measures	Verification	Assumptions
If-then	implement a new workflow paradigm—>	Foster innovation while practicing good teamsmanship—>	position CCC for even greater Spirit-empowered impact (esp. 10yr/Vision 15k/— connecting people to life-defining relationships in Christ ->	
			4 types: direct, leading, proxy, unobtrusive	
1	**Project Goal (what)**			presenting problem: no dependable rhythm in which to dream, plan, and execute. Leads to initiators sense of stagnation and support sense of overwhelm.
	Move from "always on-always open" to 2 seasons of plan/work per year.	using new paradigm by 9/1 with full implementation by Jan19	[direct] Asana project	
2	**ProjectPurpose (in order to...)**			
	Gain ministry-wide ability to envision and enact while fostering both ministry health and Spirit-responsiveness			
3	**Project Outcomes (deliverables/enhanced relationships or rhythms)**			
	CCC staff and key volunteers understand and live within 2 horizon framework	1. >80% "understand" or "understand well" after training. 2) <10% "outside parameters" for ministry year 1819	1. [direct] post-training survey. 2. [direct] post-use support data	
	"Gatekeepers" experience balance of responsibility and authority	General reflection of ability to do job	[indirect] annual review question	
	Initiator's experience an eager partnership while Smin experiences ability to project and supply	80% both parties reflect "excellent" or "good" on collaboration score	[direct] Ministry Year 1819 survey (May 2019)	
	A scalable and sustainable workflow for CCC			
4	**Project Inputs (tasks, when, how much, whom)**			
	develop wkflow ideas and visuals	v1 6/12; v2 8/8; v3 8/15	Asana project	
	Revise event/use standards with common redirects, available digitally	14-Aug	Asana project	
	intro and train staff and volunteers	21-Aug	Asana project	
	live gauges for immediate feedback	19-Nov	separate Asana project	indirectly related
	vet and decide on sched/fac mgmt tool-system	19-Nov	separate Asana project	indirectly related

Appendix B

Ministry Rhythm Visuals

Here are three tools we've developed as an approach to a Calendar 3.0. Some have been cropped for page size limitations. You can download a scalable PDF at waynecstewart.com/flowimages.

Image 1 is an Excel sheet that flows as a "modified waterfall" from top

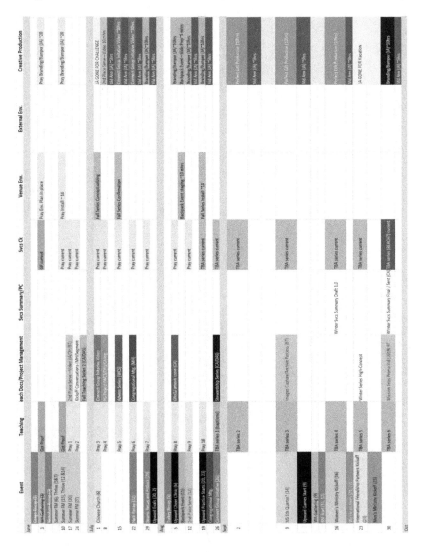

Image 2 is one week in our Cal 3.0 (Asana):

Cal3 2020A (Jan-Jun)
List   Board   Timeline   Calendar   Progress   Forms   More...

Task name	Assignee	Due date ↓	Ops Status	Weekly Comm	AV Status
Thao Ha and Daniel Goebel Wedding 3	igiammalgu c	Jan 3 2020 - Jan 4 2020		No Comm	Completed (11)
......Jan 1/5-1/11......... 1		Saturday	Call		
Next Steps Jan20 1 ... 3	Marci Hende	Sunday			
AF Restart 3 ... 2	Kyle Bartholic	Sunday		No Comm	No AV
HS Core Restart 2	Kyle Bartholic	Sunday		No Comm	No AV
MS Core Restart 1 ... 2	Nate Hellum	Sunday		No Comm	No AV
Welcome Teaching Series 1 ... 3	Chris Akers	Sunday		Completed	Budgeted AV
Wachter Visit	RECAP	adummmic...	Sunday		Completed	AV Basic
Finance 101 2 ... 2	Marci Hende	Jan 7 2020		Completed	AV Basic
Catalyst Rehearsals (begin) 3 ... 3	Chris Akers	Jan 7 2020		No Comm	Budgeted AV
Classic Choir Restart 7 ... 3	Chris Akers	Jan 8 2020		Completed	
Caffeine in Chaos Restart 2 ... 1	mmcdowell	Jan 8 2020		Completed	No AV
Men I Connect Restart 5 ... 2	Aaron Roth...	Jan 8 2020		Completed	Completed
Wednesday Night Live Restart 1 ... 3	Nate Hellum	Jan 8 2020		Completed	Budgeted AV
Digging Deeper into Philippians 9 ... 2	mmcdowell	Jan 9 2020		Completed	AV Basic
Women I Connect Bible Study 10 ... 2	mmcdowell	Jan 9 2020		Completed	AV Basic
Classic Worship Rehearsals in G2 5 ... 3	Chris Akers	Jan 9 2020		No Comm	Budgeted AV

Image 3 is our Strategic Communication worksheet (StratComm):

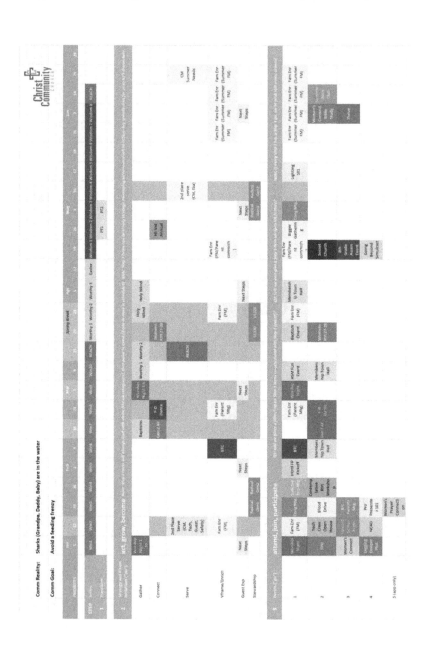

Image 4 is our current outline for event consults:

○ Event Consult

Subtasks

- ○ PCR: reservation block date(s) and time(s) correct
- ○ PCR: public calendar yes/no and correct
- ○ PCR: rooms resources correct and notes added
- ○ PCR: "off dates" deleted
- ○ AV category confirmed
- ○ PCR: ops-av tag
- ○ Comm: precomm tasks reviewed | confirmed
- ○ Comm: comm plan reviewed | confirmed
- ○ Event Materials: Church Media Squad coaching
- ○ Event Ready offered
- ○ Event Ready: if waived, note in Cal2 event task and ops-lock tag in PCR | if accepted schedule and invite via Outlook
- ○ Volunteer Needs: is there a significant need to recruit volunteers

Appendix C

Brief Selected Bibliography

Ellis, Colin D. The Project Book. Wiley & Sons, 2019.

Rainer, Thom S., and Eric Geiger. Simple Church. B&H Publishing Group, 2006.

Rainer, Thom S., and Ed Stetzer. Transformational Church. B&H Books, 2010.

Schmidt, Terry. Strategic Project Management Made Simple. John Wiley & Sons, 2009.

Stanley, Andy, and Lane Jones, and Reggie Joiner. Seven Practices of Effective Ministry. Multnomah Publishing, 2008.

Wimberly, John W. The Business of The Church : The Uncomfortable Truth that Faithful Ministry Requires Effective Management. Rowman & Littlefield Publishers, 2011.

Zscheile, Dwight. The Agile Church: Spirit-Led Innovation in an Uncertain Age. Morehouse Publishing, 2017.

Other references:

A Process for Process. The Bureau Briefing Podcast with Guest Robert Sfeir, May 24 2018.

https://bureauofdigital.com/radio/bureau-briefing-content/2018/5/24/a-process-for-process

Notes:

1. Strengths, weaknesses, opportunities, threats.
https://en.wikipedia.org/wiki/SWOT_analysis

2. Wimberly Jr., John W. The Business of the Church. Rowman & Littlefield Publishers. Kindle Edition.

3. A Process for Process. The Bureau Briefing Podcast with Guest Robert Sfeir, May 24 2018. https://bureauofdigital.com/radio/bureau-briefing-content/2018/5/24/a-process-for-process

4. Can I briefly encourage you to push a little harder through the conundrum of "problem to be solved or tension to be managed?"

It's a fine question to ask. As long as you're answering the question of systems problems through the lens of systems solutions. Using a spiritual leadership filter to assess a systems challenge is a bit like taking a pocket knife to a chainsaw wood-sculpting contest. We're very likely to give up and just ignore the unfinished log. Thus, we lean maybe too much on "tension to be managed." Don't get me wrong, the phrase is an invaluable help. Let's just use it with a more refined aim.

5. A quick word about capacities. They're real. For people and organizations. While we should exercise care and rigor in measurement and interpretation, ignoring this basic fact has produced more personal burnout and church fracture than we will likely ever know. Your team wants to give everything they have. It's not fair to ask for more than everything.

6. https://en.wikipedia.org/wiki/Project_management

7. Ellis, Colin D. The Project Book (p. 6). Wiley. Kindle Edition.

8. ibid. The Project Book (p. xiv). Wiley. Kindle Edition.

9. While this as a more traditional sequential structure, the addition of a few tests or "minimum viable product" moments in Phase 3 could allow for a more agile (the preferred current structure across many arenas—esp. software development) approach. Given most church's unfamiliarity with pm on the whole, this four-phase skeleton will serve well while allowing a certain level of experimentation and learning without introducing chaos. The specific issue of pm in a church is likely to benefit from more structure than less. Still, the question of a broadly agile approach to ministry is interesting for sure. For a good primer see The Agile Church: Spirit-Led Innovation in An Uncertain Age (Dwight J. Zscheile, 2014).